THEY GOT THE GOLD MINE and
WE GOT THE SHAFT
1% vs 99%

By Diane Hamby

Dedication

This book is dedicated to those people here, there and everywhere who want a better world for everyone.

There are only two dates on our gravestones.. The day we were born and the day we die. We can decide what legacy we want to leave and what our epitaph will say. I want mine to say that "she tried everything to make sure this world was better for all children and grandchildren."

Table of Contents

Preface

They got the gold mine and we get the shaft, the 1% of our America <u>versus</u> the 99% which is the rest of us.

We were taught, from the time we were little tots that stealing is wrong and you will be punished if you do it. If you lied your reputation would be ruined and you could be charged with fraud. Committing a crime with a gun is a felony and you could serve a long time in jail. These are the rules you and I live by.

The owners of the gold mine (the 1%) live under a very different set of rules. That is why we are so angry.

There are 99% of us left out in this economy. We are looking at the greatest income disparity ever recorded in this country. It is not by accident. As more people gather in more places across the country and they share their stories. It is obvious that they all share a common thread. You have done all the right things to be successful, worked hard, went to good schools, excelled in school and yet the ladder of success has been pulled out of your reach. Those who were on the ladder are suddenly thrown off the ladder and that ladder is pulled out of their reach. None of this was by accident or your fault. All of this resulted from the deliberate actions and policies of the 1%.

This is why 99% of Americans are so angry. The owners of the gold mine (the 1%) who live under different rules have committed terrible, horrendous crimes. That 1 % lied to investors, mismanaged, gambled trillions of dollars in public and private funds. No one, not even one person has been charged with a crime. Our prisons are full of people who stole a lot less and are serving life sentences. The owners of the gold mine have ruined the world economy. They have destroyed millions and millions of lives and the dreams of millions of young adults. They have devastated young adults all over the world. They have no good future thanks to the owners of the gold mine. These crimes were committed with computers. Meanwhile the owners of the goldmine are laughing all the way to their second homes, flying their jets wherever they want to with the bail out money we gave them. Apparently it is not enough, they want more.

Many of us have spent the last three decades advancing our careers, raising families, paying down mortgages, volunteering to make our communities better places, saving for retirement, putting our children thru college. We were doing all the things we thought we should be doing to live a good life.

Meanwhile a tiny sliver of our population figured an easier way to get the gold mine and keep it for a very long time. They spent their money and resources investing in politicians. All kinds of them, federal, state, all kinds of judges and think tanks to train them. We have all watched Washington DC this year. It is more than clear to the rest of us who these politicians work for. It is not you and me.

If you are not angry, you are not paying attention. All throughout history all over the world there have been groups who always try to game the system in their favor.

This is our time to change what must be changed. Fundamental change always comes from the bottom up, not the top down. The hero we all have been waiting for is in the mirror. Thank you for realizing this.

Diane Hamby

~ ~ ~

Chapter 1

The Beginning

Knowing how the 99% of us got here will help all of us. None of what has been going on for the past thirty years was by chance. This has been the deliberate and careful actions of a small group of people. They planted the seeds many, many years ago, and they have been tending this crop and now we can see the fruits of their labor all around us.

A great many pundits, talking heads, columnists and political wonks never really agree on the exact moment when the GOP decided that this "democracy thing" just left way too much to chance. The leaders of the conservative movement realized that they needed to think strategic and long term to advance their ideology.

In 1973 some very wealthy conservative business men got together and formed the Heritage Foundation to counter the growing liberal consensus that was becoming very prevalent in American. Their original goal was to have position papers for conservative politicians. With strong leadership they were becoming a very influential conservative "Think Tank". The conservative movement began with earnest with Heritage Foundation.

The progressive movement was having problems. They were being demonized for their anti-war marches, civil right marches and women's rights marches. The conservatives began their assault on those they called "liberals". This tide had to be stopped. Good grief, blacks had rights, the war was over, and women were getting more rights. The conservatives had the disgrace of Nixon and they worked hard to get the media attention off that disgrace.

Meanwhile back in North Carolina, Sen. Jesse Helms was becoming a rising star in the conservative movement. The GOP was a fractured party at the time. The old guard was firm in believing that fiscal matters, free market, free trade and small limited government was the only path forward. Emerging in the party was Jesse Helms who was mastering the art of melding social issues and conservative fiscal issues. The melding of social and economic issues was on the great strategic moves the GOP ever made. Jesse Helms was the first to do it. His Congressional Club, did extensive polling and found one of the most successful ways to raise campaign cash was to use social issues to tug at the heart of donors. It proved to be a "gold mine". His campaign did extensive polling and found willing donors all over the country who agreed with him and would help him. His tactics have been refined thru the years but all the masters of today's successful GOP campaigns rely on the methods he used. He was Chairman of the very powerful Foreign Relations Committee, a seat he used to his advantage. Lots of important businesses realized the power he had. He is directly responsible for getting tax codes changed so his wealthy donors could take their business's off shore and bring back those cheaper goods tax free. He literally shot every textile and furniture worker in North Carolina in the hip pocket as they were leaving the polling places after voting for him. Because Helms kept convincing the voters of North Carolina that he was protecting them from the evil liberals. You know them the ones who convinced voters were out to takes their guns, kill their babies and give their jobs to black people. Oh wait, that tactic is still used today by the GOP that is how enduring these issues are, they kept Jesse in office for years the whole time millions of their jobs (Jockey, Hanes, Burlington, Thomasville, Playtex, etc.) were going offshore.

The voters of North Carolina never realized that a vote for him was a vote to end their way of life. Jesse Helms knew from the extensive polling data that his team used that he could get the good decent folks of North Carolina to vote against their own economic security by framing his campaign in issues that they could support. He was the master of manipulating voters. His method of getting people to vote against their own best interest has been taken to a higher level in today's political climate. All the money spent on think tanks, polling, linguistics, messaging, and training politicians in the art of delivery has paid off. The conservatives on the national level noticed that convincing voters to vote against their own best interest was the best return on their investment they could have ever hoped for. Melding hot button social issues with economic issues proved to be the winning ticket to advancing the conservative ideology. They realized all of their data showed that most people vote with their heart or gut, not with their head. All they needed was a serious contender in national presidential politics to take this strategy nationwide.

Nancy Reagan really wanted her beloved Ronnie to be that presidential candidate for the GOP. He was not getting enough traction with the GOP nationally, so Nancy met with Jesse Helms (1980) and a deal was struck. Jesse anointed Ronnie ensuring that he would carry the South. He was now melding social issues with fiscal policy and took these to the national stage. The powers in the GOP establishment saw an opportunity here because Ronnie's greatest asset was that he was a very disciplined actor. He knew that delivery was more important than content. He practiced and practiced before he ever went in front of the public ensuring that he always appeared congenial, in command, reassuring and absolutely charming. His job was to convince people that he was what was needed for this time in history. It did not matter that he had all the old guard around him advising him and working in his cabinet. He knew how to run a meeting and how to get people to do what he needed to get done. He was everything that Jimmy Carter was not. If he wasn't he certainly knew how to fake it and pretend that he could. This was the beginning of stacking the deck in their favor for a very long time.

The conservatives still needed good reliable voters to vote for their politicians. Anyone who has run a campaign knows this. When Rev Jerry Falwell formed the Christian Coalition, the conservatives saw an incredible opportunity to combine two powerful messaging machines. The hijacking of the Evangelical Christians by the Republican Party was a very effective move to get a sold voting block to consistently vote Republican. They had their voters, and all they had to do was talk about the issues that are near and dear to Evangelicals.

The conservatives invested heavily in all types of media, Radio, newspapers, think tanks, and of course TV. The GOP has a media machine unparalleled in the world here in America. The Fox News network is 24/7 telling viewers that the "liberal democrats" are evil and the "conservatives" are wonderful. Whenever one group wants to diminish another the tactics are the same. You define them before they define you and assail them again and again. You keep this up till you get what you want and continue it to keep it. Just like when Jesse Helms would tell the good and decent folks of North Carolina that he was looking out for them. He was really looking out for himself and his wealthy donors, while he was destroying the very livelihood of millions of his constituents.(those cheaper made textile and furniture goods could come back without paying any tariffs or taxes).

This dog and pony show went national and it is now a global problem. The 1% keep shouting that it is everybody else it to blame for the job losses here in manufacturing, when in reality they are the ones who sent those jobs overseas. Since the 2010 election the conservatives almost have everything they want. They have the Supreme Court, congress, they have their sites on the US Senate and they are working hard to take the White House. These folks like the system they have created, they are getting richer and they do not care about the Middle Class. They do not need the Middle Class to survive.

For the last 30 years the conservative messaging machine has kept the majority of voters from realizing what they have really been up to. They distract the masses with crazy hyped up stories so we couldn't see what was happening. The most famous example was that entire summer when all the media was focused on the Natalie Holloway disappearance in Aruba while the neo-cons were escalating the war in Iraq. But the public did not hear about that it was 24/7 everywhere Natalie Holloway. They have kept that same level of distraction (like using a shiny object to hypnotize) over so many things, celebrities, endless campaigns, polling, elections (when the outcomes are the ones they like). They treat the masses like simpletons who don't really care. They distort the truth with opinion, and the lies they perpetuate, so people do not trust legitimate media sources. The 1% was gaming the whole system to their advantage and they were making sure the 99% was distracted and left out. They created "survival of the richest", while telling the 99% they were really looking out for us.

" All throughout history certain groups always try to game the system, this time is no different we just need to right this wrong. The

Arab spring has shown all of us what the Arab countries have done with the economic disparity. The middle eastern countries rich with oil that so few benefit from have had enough of their 1% gaming their system against the 99%. They seem to get more international attention than protesters in this country who are fighting the same economic injustices. Why is the conservative messaging media machine not giving them the press they deserve? Maybe they don't want you focused on them and their message...

~ ~ ~

Chapter 2

Free Market - The truth

Let's start by exposing the biggest lies that have gotten here. You hear conservatives sing from all the conservative media outlets. You know them, Fox News, conservative columnists, Rush Limbaugh, presidential candidates and on all the conservative think tank websites "Free Market", they polled and polled till the found the words that the most people would support. Of course people ought to be able to sell a good or services without out all those silly regulations.

Let's start with the best example that everyone needs to pay attention too. The illegal drug trade, operates in the true "free market" realm. There are no silly regulations to say that the drugs are what people are paying for, and they are sold for whatever price the buyers can get. They can do whatever ever they want to get market share. That is what "free market" means.

Let's look closely at this illegal drug trade and see what is the good side of this "free market" model. A very few people (drug lords) earn an extraordinary amount of money. Anybody who doesn't like the way the drug lords do business can be eliminated, killed, maimed or their family members hurt. Just like in the old west or during prohibition. They can sell a product that has absolutely no safety standards. It could kill, maim, seriously injure whoever takes them, and that is wonderful. Because they operate in that "free market." The dealers selling the illegal drugs can sell them for whatever price they want. So they start selling them cheap to get people addicted and then they keep raising prices. After all it is a "free market", that is what you can do.

So conservatives keep screaming that we need to get rid of all those silly regulations that are keeping business's from hiring and keeping them from competing in that "free market"" world, Let's look at some of those pesky regulations.

Let's start with the obvious one. Imagine if automobile makers didn't have to build their cars with safety in mind. The Big Three automakers could do whatever they wanted to just to make money. Those cars could be unsafe or could be a gas guzzler, things would not have to work like advertised. Automakers could charge whatever they wanted. Under the "free market" system the buyer would not have any recourse if anything when wrong.

What if homebuilders operated in the "free market" world. Contractors could build a house however they wanted. Contractors wouldn't have to deal with those pesky building codes. The codes that make a house safe to live in, the wiring safe to use, with the plumbing that works. What difference will it make not to have codes, sure they say it's safe, but under "free market" they would not have to build it to a standard and heaven help us that some government official inspect it to make sure they did build it to a uniform code. Image skyscrapers built in the "free market" world. I surely would not work or live in one.

What if restaurants did not have to comply with sanitary codes. Restaurants could be as clean or a filthy as owners wanted. You could eat there and maybe get sick or not. You know those pesky sanitary regulations are hindering them from making money.

Do you see a trend here? Those regulations are a hindrance for making money, but not a hindrance from keeping the public safe from greedy, unscrupulous business practices. There are lots of places in the world that have the "free market" economy. They are called "third world countries."

So why do the conservatives blast from every outlet they can that we need "free market?" The main goal is profit by any means. Conservatives believe greed is good and people who are rich need to be constantly rewarded for figuring out how to game the system by being made richer, by whatever means necessary to get there. Hence to them using the "free market" is fine because it makes the rich richer and exploits the rest of us. Conservatives just figure the poor deserve to be poor because they haven't figured out how to be rich. Sure does make it easier to exploit the poor if you think they deserve to be poor.

Let's really look at all the consequences of this "free market" thinking and why they are really pushing for it. In Third World countries (Honduras, Viet Nam, Mexico) where "free market" is the law of the land. Nobody pays taxes so there is no government to make regulations of any kind. Therefore there are no pesky regulators. What really annoys the conservatives is our tax system, because it really hinders "free market" policies. In the US we have a 90% compliance rate on taxes. (90% of business and individuals pay taxes and file returns) Giving America the ability to regulate companies and protect our citizens. Not only do we have regulations (gasp) we have regulators (gasp, gasp) to enforce them. Third World countries don't have that ability. All the Third World country businesses don't have to worry about those pesky environmental regulations. They can freely pollute the water, the air, the ground. They can do whatever they want to make the most money with the least input. Workers are expendable. Third World countries that have unregulated markets are haven for those who believe greed is good and that is all that matters. Profit is all the motivation they need.

The conservatives (Fox News, Rush Limbaugh, Beck, GOP Presidential candidates) keep chanting that all those regulations here are stopping the economy from growing. Companies are just so hindered from hiring. Let's really look at what they are saying. The regulations are protecting all of us against corporate greed. Imagine if that plastics company on the edge of town did not have to be careful with their waste. The company could just dump all that waste in the local creek that just happens to run into the local reservoir. The company owners wouldn't have to pay minimum wage, they can hire people and pay workers whatever they want. The company wouldn't have to have any safety equipment, so what if the workers get hurt, maimed or even killed. What is the big deal if they were really smart they would be a boss not an employee and wouldn't get hurt. We cannot work is this country for less than minimum wage, or go backwards with regulations that keep all of us safe, just so unscrupulous corporate profiteering can go unchecked.

In this country our water is generally very safe to drink. We have national clean water standards that keep us safe. We have national food safety standards. You can buy food in any grocery store, fast food restaurants, little neighborhood grills, school cafeterias, and numerous other places. Those national standards keep us from getting sick and ending up in the hospital from unsanitary conditions. Try eating food and drinking the water in Third World countries. You could end up extremely ill or even dead. We have clean air standards, so we can breathe our air without becoming ill from respiratory problems. All things that discharge into the air, water and land come under our regulations. Think how much more money corporations could make if they did not have to comply with those basic regulations. These regulations keep our water safe to drink, food safe to eat and air safe to breathe. They also keep us safe from unscrupulous corporate profiteering.

Third World countries have a "free market", because those few people who are extremely wealthy keep the rest of the population from doing better. They make sure that there is only a shadow government to hinder what they do best. Their goal is to keep making as much money as possible however they can and not letting anybody or anything stop them.

So the conservative media machine screams that all these pesky regulations are keeping businesses from hiring. That is why the economy is doing badly. It is a deliberate smoke screen to get all of us to let them exploit our resources, communities and workers just so the few can keep making a great deal of money. If this was true Third World (Mexico, Viet Nam) countries would be booming. When in fact that is not what is happening in Third World countries. They are still very much Third World countries. No matter how many sweat shops employ people, most of the people are very, very poor and a very few are extremely rich. So this is the vision for America that the conservatives are shouting for us to do. For this "free market" to really work for them you have to get rid of all those pesky government regulations and regulators. You know the people who check to make sure food is safe, buildings are safe, roads and bridges are safe and employees are safe. So if you destroy the government's ability to enforce these regulations you will end up with "free market" by default.

For this "free market" to really work we would have to have very limited government or no government. There are two ways to get there. Bankrupt the government by spending our money on things that really drain the account, like two wars, a drug giveaway, and cutting revenue (taxes on the wealthiest). If you cut revenue and increase spending you will run out of money quicker.

The 1% who will stand to benefit the most from "free markets" will keep singing it every chance they get. After all the corporate owners, bankers, stock brokers and the 1% are just trying to get richer. That is what they all do.

Conservatives and their media machine will just keep howling for somehow in this Utopia they seem to forget a few basic principles of markets. All successful economies share a few basic principles that benefit everybody. They have a well regulated banking industry. All successful economies have that. They have a well regulated stock market. Businesses have to be able to raise capital, thru selling stocks or borrowing money. But those banks and stocks have to be well regulated, so you got to have regulators. You have to have Commerce laws and people to enforce them. All successful economies have a "Fair Market" system in place. That is the only way that Third World countries become successful economies, by implementing those business and government practices that make markets "fair" not "free". So while selfish, profiteering conservatives are shouting "free market" those of us who understand what economies need to be successful is "fair markets".

The difference between those two markets is the distance between a modern economy and a third world economy. When you hear the conservative media machine singing about "free markets", tell them to go ahead and go to a third world country and do whatever the market there will let them. If businesses are going to do business here, it needs to be in "fair market." We have had to pick up the pieces of our economy after their unregulated banking and stock disasters. There was not enough regulation to keep the banks, insurance companies and brokerage firms from collapsing the world economies. Many countries are still very weak from this deregulating of the banks. We are still trying to recover from the conservative "free market" system. Remind them of this. Remember these simple truths when you go to vote.

~~~

Chapter 3

Free Trade - The Truth

Here we have another one of those phrases that sound great "free trade." The conservatives make it sound so simple. Why can't companies sell whatever they have to sell wherever they want? Tariffs (taxes) are unfair and take away from profit. Never mind that workers were exploited and companies had the goods to sell. Never mind that all these trade agreements are meant to protect somebody from unfair trade practices, from goods that are subsidized by governments (corn ,wheat, soybeans).

They want us to believe that it is okay to send companies off shore to where people make $50 per month sewing clothes, and when the goods come back here with no tariffs against stuff made from people $8 hr. They still charge like that person is making $8 bucks per hour, and guess where the difference goes. Aren't corporate profits wonderful?Remember international corporations are smart enough to game the system. They need to be rewarded with more tax breaks and giveaways. So they can get richer. They keep slamming us with rhetoric that "free trade" is the answer to what our economy needs now.

When the conservatives promoted all this "free trade" they kept saying it would open up new markets for American goods and life would be wonderful for all. Except the opposite has happened, with "free trade", it has destroyed the way of life for industrialized nations around the world. It has given those who can exploit poor workers in third world countries, to make goods extremely cheap. "Free trade" means there are no regulations to control the flow of goods across borders.

What "free trade" has really done is made it so easy for corporations (Hanes , Nike, Jockey, Thomasville ,Cannon, etc.) to close plants here in American and take those manufacturing jobs to where labor is really cheap. So sure enough cheap goods came back here and it has been going on long enough that when the goods are still cheap, people without jobs can't afford them. That is what has happened here in American. "Free trade" has given corporations (Hanes, Nike, Thomasville , Cannon ,etc.) the ability to exploit desperate workers all across the globe. While there are no trade laws protecting the goods that are still made here in America. When you go to Wal-Mart , Target, K Mart, there are hardly any goods made here in America any more. The familiar brands made by companies that use to be in our communities are off shore. Cannon Mills the makers of sheets and towels employed thousands of workers here in North Carolina, when Wal-Mart told the owners to send the manufacturing overseas to make it cheaper and the owners said no. They wanted to keep all those good manufacturing jobs in America. Wal-Mart responded by not buying their goods anymore, and Cannon Mills was forced to close with their biggest customer gone. Those workers in China and other Asian markets still do not make a living wage, and the actual goods are not that much cheaper to us consumers and certainly not the quality we were use to. More profit for the greedy and a lot less jobs and money for workers.

The conservative politicians made sure that when they were writing all those "free trade" agreements that there would be no taxes due when the cheap goods came back here. So the corporations (Hanes , Nike, Jockey, Thomasville, etc.) who have gamed the system are still getting richer while all the workers here who are out of work and no hope of replacing those jobs. They have destroyed the middle class here in American with their "free trade" policies that they are still promoting.

What we needed all along was "fair trade". The kind of trade that sustains economy's, not drains them. Since they gamed the whole system it will be hard to change it, but not impossible. "Fair trade" would have made those cheaply made goods more competitive when they came here. Our goods would have remained competitive. There would also be an incentive to have goods made here, instead of the greed of the few destroying the livelihood of the many. The conservatives keep singing that this is not what would happen, but of course just because they chant "free trade" will never make it "fair trade".

The few are doing extremely well under "free trade" want more of it in more places. Because they know there are desperate people all over the planet they want to exploit. They want to find cheaper labor, because workers in China want to live better. The workers in Indonesia want better. Workers in India wants to live better, so they keep looking for ever cheaper labor. Do you see a pattern here? The few only care about making a great deal of money at the expense of the many.

Let's look at China as an example. Corporations here (Hanes ,Nike, Jockey, Thomasville, etc.) move over there to use the cheap labor and then bring it back here. Sounds like a win win, except again a very few are making a great deal, and the many workers are loosing their jobs here. If we had "fair trade" those goods would have to pay some sort of tax so there would be an incentive for companies to stay here. But since companies spend their money to influence the congress, they line their own pockets instead of workers and the middle class looses. If you make a good here you cannot sell it to China without paying a huge tariff. We do not do the same when their stuff comes here. That is that "free market" again, where only a few benefit.

When you hear all those conservatives and their media messaging machine promoting "free trade", have them give you examples of where exactly on the planet it works? Ask," where is the middle class?" Now there are lots of countries that practice "fair trade" and they have a sustainable middle class. (Norway, Germany, Denmark, Sweden) The conservative ideology does not believe in a middle class. They only believe in winners and losers and they not care about anybody in between. Once you understand that you will understand why this is the system they want to have here.

~ ~ ~

Chapter 4

Trickle Down Economics - what it really is

This nonsense started under Ronald Reagan, and the conservatives are still preaching and practicing it. The conservatives have been saying that if you keep pouring money into the top 1% (those in the top income brackets) it will trickle down to everybody else. This is a made up economic theory. This is the silliest economic nonsense that the conservative messaging machine keeps preaching. Somehow they think the more they say something the more it makes it true. They are hoping that spreading this empty ridiculous theory will make it true. If it was even remotely possible, we would all live in McMansions and drive cool new SUV's. Instead the exact opposite has happened. The 1% has increased their incomes 277% in the last thirty years and the rest of us have lost ground, stagnant wages and all of our costs have gone up.

The top 1% has sucked the rest of us dry. They have quadrupled their incomes, while the rest of us have lost income over the last 30 years.

That is how this pouring of our money into the top 1% really works in our economy and economies around the globe have been devastated by this practice. Even though this economic theory is a proven lie, our congress still practices this policy. They keep pouring so much of the public treasury into the top 1%, the banks, the brokerage firms, insurance companies, oil companies and their drug companies. The conservative messaging machine keeps telling all of us that this is how you get the economy moving.

So you have to ask why are they still doing it? Trying to sell the 1% as the "job creators", don't tax them. There is a very obvious answer, because that top 1% controls the politics of most of the free world democracies, and certainly those countries that are not democracies.

Everyone living in America or any other democracy will have to face this truth. As long as our politicians have to raise extraordinary amounts of money to run for public office, this happens they will have to do what the 1% wants. When our Supreme Court says that it is okay for corporations to donate to campaigns, any amount and not disclose donors, they made this corruption legal. The question we all need to ask, is this practice ethical?

Our politicians are working for the people who give them money to run for office, and now these politicians have to do things that benefit those donors. You end up with the system we have now. Even though the conservatives keep screaming that his isn't so, it is so. Look closely and you see how the 1% are benefitting and the 99% are the losers.

Let's look at the most extreme example of corporate welfare to the top 1%. The classic example of pouring our money into the top 1% while saying it will benefit all of us. When the economy was starting to collapse in August of 2007 thru April of 2010, the Federal Reserve administered the largest bailout in US history (without congressional approval) and without any oversight or stipulations. Our federal government bailed out the banking giants to the tune of 7.7 trillion dollars. Yes 7.7 trillion dollars folks. And what has this money gotten us in return? What has the banks done to show their gratitude to the American people. They were engaged in risky financial transactions and were in danger of going insolvent and leading to a major financial meltdown. So they thanked us(banks) laid off thousands and thousands of workers forever, gave their CEO's millions and millions in bonuses, and stopped lending money to business's and people who wanted to borrow. Not only did they not use this unearned money (welfare) to keep the economy moving by lending that money and keeping people employed, they used that money to influence more politicians to keep getting federal dollars at no interest!!!!!!!! They are still arguing about letting people collect unemployment checks because they think it is welfare and gives the wrong message. That 7.7 trillion was not small change and they are still ungrateful about it and say if we don't stop pouring money in they will collapse the economy. They keep this threat up especially when there is talk about stricter regulations to keep them from getting into financial trouble again.

When congress keeps giving tax breaks to the top 1% that is also welfare. They did not earn this money, it is welfare. They are pouring our public funds into the top 1% preaching that trickle down will work. When what it is really doing is giving unearned money to them. It is the most expensive welfare in America. Unearned money has no value to the person you give it to. Whether it is a wall street broker, too big to fail bank, banker, a corporate owner or a dead beat relative. They always use the unearned money for things that they want never for things they need. So what has the top 1% used their welfare checks for? They have used them to buy more lobbyist and politicians so they can get more free stuff. They used those welfare checks to buy News Corporations, TV Stations, Think Tanks, newspapers, talking heads, columnists, all sorts of media outlets and personnel to keep saying how wonderful "trickle down" is. They have not created any jobs, they have not help the economy moving. They haven't built new plants, hired more workers. They have bought more vacation homes, yachts, planes and baubles.

The conservatives tell all sorts of stories and things to say to try to convince us that his is sound economic policy. The 1% have been getting these welfare checks for over 30 years and they have been getting bigger. So if we the 99% are going to pull these squealing pigs from the public trough we need to be ready. This is not going to be a pretty sight, and they are not going to leave the trough willingly. The 1% do not want to give up their welfare, and they certainly don't want to pay their fair share. They have been getting a free ride for 30 years. They have enjoyed all the benefits of our society, banking regulations, infrastructure, public services and educated people to work for them, and the public servants when they need them. The 1% have not contributed enough money to let anyone else to go to this trough, and like all pigs being forced to do things they don't want to do the squealing is going to get louder and louder.

When you hear the preaching on "trickle down" ask them to show an economy where this works. Because every Third World country has the same policies (1% elite moneyed class and the very poor 99%) and they never seem to do any better. They are all still very much third world and never emerge to a thriving economy.

Don't back down, keep questioning the reasoning behind this economic policy. Because the statistics clearly show that only a few do great and the rest of the population does very poorly .Every leading economist has done graphs showing the income disparity of the 1% vs the 99%. They only disagree on why it is happening, not on whether or not it is happening. Of course remember that conservatives only care about winners, they do not care about how many losers and they surely do not believe in the middle class.

This economic policy has almost destroyed the middle class in America and in many other industrialized nations. Moderate republicans use to call it "voodoo economics" but they are being drowned out by the conservative media messaging machine trying in vain to convince us that trickle down creates jobs and we must continue this practice or the "job creators" will collapse the economy.

~ ~ ~

Chapter 5

Taxes - the truth and their lies

Conservatives (led by Grover Norquist, and Citizens for Tax Reform) and their media machine keep preaching that all taxes are evil. Unless someone else pays them (99% and the (1%) get the benefits. Oh wait that is what happens now. Let's have a good look at taxes. Which is the money we all pay (federal, state, and local taxes) so we can have all the services and infrastructure that make our lives, safer, better and easier.

Tax money is what pays those school teachers, fireman, policemen, paramedics, all military personnel, food inspectors, traffic controllers, highway patrol, FBI, forest rangers and the list goes on and on.

Tax money pays for and clean water system and waste treatment facilities, roads, airports, sea ports all sorts of things that make it easier for us to go to work, have business's, go anywhere we want to or have to. Everyone benefits from these. Third World countries can't provide these services or infrastructure because they do not have a system in place for collecting taxes. That is why they are Third World countries and have so many living in poverty.

When terrible disasters happen, it is our tax money that provides relief, immediate help, and loans to rebuild. The earthquakes in California, devastating hurricanes in the south and east, floods (all kinds), crippling snows, crippling ice storms that destroy utility lines. These disasters overwhelm state budgets, and only the Federal government (FEMA to the rescue) can help. It is our tax money that provides the relief and help.

Who builds all these roads so you and I can travel? Who pays for the roads that send our goods wherever we want to? Who builds our airports so we can travel the world? Who builds the seaports for our goods to go around the world? Who protects our ports when ships come from all over the globe? The federal government builds the roads, the airports, seaports and makes them safe with our tax money and all of our lives are better for it.

Third World countries do not have all these things. Their inability to form a stable government, and to collect taxes are why they are Third World countries. Look at Somalia where a small band of pirates terrorize a major international shipping lane and there is not Somalian government to stop them. There is no structure, no economy to employ these people. The only way they have to make money is to pirate the seas. All businesses that use that lane are paying dearly for that lack of government in one little country. Seems like we get a lot for our tax money. So you have to wonder why taxes are so evil? It is actually pretty easy to figure out. If a small group of people want their "free market", "free trade", "trickle down" our government and tax system is ruining this "survival of the richest" policy that the 1% want to keep in place.

The conservative politicians (Boehner, Paul Ryan, Eric Cantor, all the GOP Presidential candidates) try very hard from all their media sources to convince the masses that taxes, any kind, especially taxes on the top 1% are evil. They almost had people convinced, till they collapsed the world economy from their unregulated banking and brokerage firms. So many people were affected, so many had to rely on the Federal government for services, unemployment benefits, social security, medicare, food stamps and never mind everyone is still using all that public infrastructure to get around and to look for jobs.

American voters have realized how important the Federal government is to our everyday lives. Voters know their tax money pays for those highways, snow removal, airports, storm clean up, policeman, fireman, teachers and we need to have these services to continue. We need all those government workers who make our lives better. So reason has prevailed and hopefully will transcend this nonsense. The conservative media messaging machine still keeps preaching taxes are evil and we need more tax cuts for the rich The politicians who are working for the 1% who fund their campaigns have to keep these lies alive. The 1% need to have more "trickle down", "free market" to happen and definitely need to advance more "free trade" that destroys more American jobs.

The " taxes hurt the economy" mantra has been taken to a whole new level by the extreme right conservatives. Most every republican politician on the Federal and State level have signed a pledge from Grover Norquist (Americans for Tax Reform) stating that they will never, no never raise taxes for any reason. Grover Norquist believes taxes hurt the economy and he wants to take away all power of the federal government except to keep the rich richer.

Remember if these folks are going to continue with "survival of the richest", "free market", "trickle down", and "free trade" they have to really weaken the Federal government. He believes the only function the government ought to have is make the rich richer. Just like all those Third World countries(1% wealthy and 99%very poor) around the world. This pledge is very real. This pledge that these conservative politicians are signing, they are putting this ahead of the pledge they take when they are sworn in to uphold the Constitution of the United States of America. Never mind that to truly solve any crisis you must be able to use every tool imaginable to solve the problem. The mentality of these republicans has been reduced to (we will do everything "except raise revenues") I am sure that their stable of lawyers they have trained and groomed are telling them that signing this pledge is legal, but nowhere in reality is it ethical. Imagine your doctor telling you in a serious health crisis he would do everything he could, except what would probably save your life.

Why don't we hear more this? If democrats were all signing a pledge that took away their rights to govern effectively, and they were putting that pledge ahead of their upholding the Constitution we would never hear the end of it. The republicans and their media messaging machine would make the democrats lives a living hell. They would keep chanting over and over that it was illegal and they could find lots of conservative lawyers and judges to say so and pretty soon the democrats would be run out of office. But that is not what is happening to the republicans .You recently saw on 60 minutes that Norquist has been doing this for twenty years. Hardly any American knows about Norquist and his pledge that can make or break a republican politician. That just proves how much of the media machine they control.

Remember that Third World countries have no tax structure, no government regulations and people try hard to flee those countries everyday. So why do the conservatives messaging machine and the 1% they work for want America to be a Third World country? That is where we are headed if they continue to try to bankrupt the US Treasury and defund the government. Why do the 1% (wealthy class) want the "free market" of a third world country? Ask this question again and again. Because they will be richer than they are now.

When our government collects a tax and pays for services it provides it is the most sound of economic policies. Every state and local government does this, it is called "Pay as you Go," which is pretty self explanatory. Tax and spend is "pay as you go".

What the conservative republicans have done is borrow and spend for years. Under their hero Reagan who started the cutting taxes and living on borrowed money instead of "pay as you go", since he took office in 1980 and we are still using the public credit card. Now the conservatives and the 1% they work for do not want anybody to pay the credit card bill that is long overdue. Meanwhile the conservatives and the 1 % they work for keep using the credit card to pay for two wars and drug companies give a ways. Spending and borrowing is the policy that will bankrupt this country. If you or I just lived on credit cards we could probably successfully do it for maybe 18months maximum till we had no more credit. As long as a government agency has taxing authority (which creditors look at the ability to pay) they can borrow money. When congress keeps saying they won't raise the debt ceiling and won't pay then other governments will stop lending us money and then we will have to go to "pay as you go". That will be very painful. Borrow and spend is what is driving the huge deficits.

~ ~ ~

Chapter 6

Social Security -the truth - and why the conservatives hate it!

Why do the conservatives hate Social Security so much? Because it helps the middle class and the poor have a little bit of security in their old age. When Social Security was enacted in 1938 the biggest group living in poverty was old folks. Most people did not earn a retirement from the company they worked for. Those who farmed certainly did not make enough to save for retirement, especially with the uncertainty of farming. When they could no longer work and they had no way to sustain themselves and their families. The conservatives want all of us to believe that people have not earned a secure retirement. I personally work very hard physically and I pay a great deal into Social Security, and to listen to the conservatives demean me because I expect to collect on what I have rightfully paid into, is ludicrous. They call it a "Ponzi scheme", and they try to make entitlement sound evil.

We pay into Social Security, we have earned it. If you do not pay into it, you are not eligible to collect. The conservatives politicians and the 1% they work for believe that someone needs to make a profit. They would rather take that money and gamble it in the stock market. They just want more money to gamble and charge outrageous brokerage fees , they really do not care if we have anything in our old age. Never mind that these same people are the ones who have gambled and lost trillions of dollars in the last 3 years. They wiped out many personal fortunes, public and private pension funds, and yet they keep screaming that the stock market is better than the Social Security system. Now you would think they would stop after losing trillions in the last three years, but the nonsense continues. Those who make their fortunes in the stock market, the ones who are making money by manipulating the stock market want new money to gamble with.

So let's look at what would happen if your parents had their retirement fund totally in the Stock Market in the last three years, and their money was now gone. Lots of people's money was there, and they did loose. Then what happens when they have no money? Do they move in with you and your family? Where do they go? What happens to the widow next door who has no living relatives? We can envision a class of homeless people like we have not seen since the Great Depression.

Most people with any common sense see thru this lie. So many people have watched their own retirement funds their friends and relatives lose all of their hard earned retirement savings. Yet this push for ending Social Security will not go away. The conservative politicians are just hoping that they will someday have the votes in congress to abolish it. All they to do is convince younger workers that it is evil and not pay into it and the fund will run out of money. This is just another example where the conservatives want to do away with anything that will help the middle class and the poor. If you have to rely on a government program they consider you weak and in a true free market system you won't survive, that is why they don't like Social Security.

Tell the GOP to stop with the nonsense. Again, look at Third World countries, they don't have Social Security and most of the population lives in poverty and the elderly in extreme poverty. Tell them that again and again you want security in your old age. Why do they want us to live like people do in Third World Countries?

Social Security is earned, it is not a form of welfare. Their other argument is to raise the retirement age to save it. The age has been raised. People who work physically hard cannot continue to work that hard well into their 70"s. While those who are gaming the system keep getting that real government welfare. This is all a smoke screen. Social Security is only paid on the first $106,000 of income. Any income over that is not subject to Social Security taxes. To keep the fund solvent, the fair thing would be to raise that cap above that amount. But the squealing pigs will not have it, they signed a pledge that says they can't or they will never be re-elected again. They certainly aren't going to pay anymore because they bought those politicians to make sure they don't pay anymore taxes. So when you hear that they want the janitor at the local mall to work into his 70's, or the carpenter next door, or the cashier at the grocery store. They keep shouting it so you won't think or notice there is a more fair way to handle this. Remember the smoke screen tactics. So when you see all those people who work physically hard for a living, the conservatives want them all to work till they drop. Just so they can have more and the rest of us pay for them to have more and we all get a lot less. They are screaming from all their media outlets that we all have to sacrifice more, more than already have. They keep getting more. Everyday a new story that the top 1% has increased their incomes by 277%, and the rest of us are losing ground. The conservatives think that this is fair, after all they are working real hard to keep "survival of the richest." The average amount a retiree collects from social security is $14,000 per year. Doesn't put them anywhere near being in the 1%.

~ ~ ~

Chapter 7

Government workers - who are they? And why do we need them

Another incredible lie, let's get rid of government workers. They are unnecessary and besides private contractors would be better.

Just imagine dialing "911"

Sir we have to have your credit card before we can proceed. So in the middle of a serious emergency you are fooling with this. " Sir, we are sorry but you do not have any available credit on that card, do you have another." Meanwhile your house is burning, somebody needs an ambulance, whatever. What happens if you don't have a card.

"We are sorry sir, but we cannot help you!"

This is the vision that the conservatives have for America.

This lie that government workers are parasites and we do not need them. Unfortunately this is happening on the State Level as states run out of money. Let's really look at what this mean. First the conservative media machine blabbers that the Federal Government does not create jobs. Really, then who do all those soldiers and military personnel work for? FBI? CIA? TSA? USDA inspectors, bridge inspector, air traffic controllers, postal worker, VA hospital workers (doctors, nurses, CNA's) and many many more vital people. Can we really live without these workers? Not safely, and there is not private agency that will do these things without charging and outrageous amount.

But the conservative media machine wants to keep deceiving the public, and the conservatives in congress are chiming we need to cut these jobs. Remember all the Third World countries they do not have any of these employees, except maybe soldiers to keep the masses in line. This lie is one of most serious that they keep spreading around. What is happening on the state level they are laying off teachers who are "state employees", highway patrol, environmental workers who keep our food and water safe, social workers and the list goes on and on. All these people make us safer, smarter and keep us competitive in a global economy. When you get rid of enough of government workers we slide ever closer to "Third World" status. It makes it a whole lot easier for the rich to exploit everything else to make more money. Do you see a trend here?

Every state that has followed this practice of cutting state employees has higher un-employment than those that did not. Their economies are stagnating. These workers buy homes, buy cars, go out to eat, go shopping and generally contribute significantly to the local economy. When you get rid of all these middle class jobs you are making the local economies stall more.

When State's gut their budget in the name of austerity (actually they are practicing "trickle down") they cut off money to local governments. Local governments are the ones who pay the fireman, policeman, paramedics, deputies, animal control, trash collectors, all sorts of people who make our lives safer and better. These people are being laid off in unprecedented numbers. It does have a snow ball effect. More good jobs lost forever, declining tax revenues, and less people to enforce all kind of regulations. These communities are now ripe to be exploited by unscrupulous companies. Oh wait, do you think maybe all this was a smoke screen to make it easier for the 1% to do their "free market" thing? Of course it is. The 1% and the conservative media machine blab one thing, just so they can do another to make themselves richer.

~ ~ ~

Chapter 8

Cutting the deficit will boost the economy - another lie

The conservative media machine and their henchman (Boehner ,Cantor, Ryan, McConnell) keep saying they have to cut the budget deficit to boost the economy. Have any of these people taken an economics class? This lie that the conservatives and their media machine keep chanting over and over is one of the most damaging to our fragile economy. Let's look at why this deception still has legs in the media. Remember the conservatives have a lot of media outlets to chant this from. If the top 1% owns the media outlets, and their main goal is to get richer at the expense of everything else, then the 1% wants this deceit continue.

If the congress and senate focus's on this, they will never be able to help the economy do better. Repeat this concept over and over. Just because the conservative media machine says it over and over, it will never make it the truth. If this is all we focus on we cannot help the economy to do better. We have already proved that when you cut all those jobs that are government jobs, it hurts the economy. There are less people paying into the tax base, and now these people need some sort of government assistance, un-employment, food stamps, social services, all sorts of things. The spending we need to cut are those huge expenses that are on borrowed money. (Two wars and drug subsidy)

If the 99% fall for this and continue to focus at this end of the problem it will only get worse. It will be self- fulfilling prophesy.

Let's give some easy examples. What would happen if every household in America and every business decided we all just needed to pay off all our debt and not spend any money on anything else except for necessities. In my house we would just use our money to pay down our mortgage, credit card and car payments. We would not do any home improvements or upgrades. We would not go shopping except for food to prepare at home. We wouldn't go out to eat or movies or any kind of recreational activity. We just have to pay down our debts. Now if everyone in the country did this, and every business. What would happen to an economy that is driven by 70% consumer spending? The economy would come to a standstill. More people out of work, more businesses closed down.

Then the other side of this problems show itself.

Let's give an easy example that even a third grader can understand. If your family makes together $1000 per week. That puts you in the middle of middle class income. Your expenses are $3000 per month. So that leaves you with $1000 to pay for everything else. All of a sudden one of you loses your job. Your income is cut in half, but your expenses are the same. You are now -$1000 per month. You really need to increase your income. But instead you start using credit cards to pay for the difference and you go a little wild and keep charging. There is now only one way out of this hole. You have to increase your income to get above water.

That is what is happening with the Federal government. Their income has been limited by the workers who are not, working and not paying taxes millions and millions have lost jobs. They also decided to give welfare to the rich (that's what cutting taxes on them is), they also put two wars on a credit card, (no war bonds), and of course the subsidies to drug companies disguised as a drug plan for the elderly. The money is still going out. You cannot close this gap with cuts alone, somehow you have to increase revenue. This is a common sense no-brainer. That incredible loud screaming conservative messaging machine keeps screaming, cuts, cuts, cuts and no increases. So they are hoping that is all we focus on. Of course they don't want to cut the things they like, just the services the other 99% of us need.

Meanwhile the conservative politicians keep cutting jobs while pledging to never, no never increase income! Maybe this is some new kind of math, because my calculator keeps showing it will get worse and worse. Maybe they have special conservative calculators that shows you will up in the black some day! Maybe they live in a different dimension, but they are certainly not operating in the real world!

So what can the Federal Government do? Lots of things, just look at what the Chinese government is doing the make sure they win the 21st century. China is making investments in roads, bridges, sea ports, railroads, education, innovation in new energy. All sorts of things that will keep them winning the 21st century. China doesn't have a conservative calculator. Even the conservative Chinese government knows they are going to have to invest to increase revenue to grow their economy. Meanwhile back here the conservatives are stuck on stupid thinking they can cut their way to prosperity. But what if they really do know this and don't care about winning the 21st century, they just want to keep their rich friends rich and keep the power they now have! If that is the case then we all ought to be really angry. (Occupy Wall Street has this anger) Again, it is the deliberate actions of the few, to keep themselves rich and powerful at the expense of the many. We will be stuck in this loop forever.

The 1% goal is to weaken the government so much, that the 99% will all just be prey for the very rich. Just like every Third World country in the world. And their messaging machine is trying to convince us this is the way it ought to be.

The conservatives have said it enough times in enough places that their number 1 goal is to make sure that the president does not get re-elected. They will do anything to make sure that happens, including keeping the economy down.

Let's look at the budget deficit issue again, this time when these conservatives held the White House. Their Vice-president Dick Cheney said again and again "DEFICITS DON'T MATTER." He said that because his administration was giving welfare to all their wealthy friends, putting both wars on the public credit card and the biggest subsidy to drug companies (calling it a drug benefit.) conservative republican politicians knew that all of this was on credit, all borrowed money, it still is. So when the 99% hear the conservatives scream that reducing the budget deficit is the number one priority seems really silly to those of us who pay attention. We need to keep playing the tape again and again of Cheney saying" deficits don't matter". If living on borrowed money was okay then, why is it not okay now? The answer is really very simple, if the conservatives really focused on creating jobs and the economy gets moving the president will be re-elected. They are actively trying to stop Obama's re-election. They have the congress now, and they have their sights on the US Senate and they really want the White House back. They know if they take it all they can fully implement "survival of the richest" and we will be doomed to losing the 21st century and could very well be well on our way to becoming an emerging "third world country"'

Just because they keep blabbing these lies, never makes them the truth. No matter how we dress up a squealing pig, they will still be squealing pigs. Tell them that again and again and again. Write, call or picket your local congressmen and Senators. Write letters to the editor. E-mail congress, keep letting your voice be heard.

~ ~ ~

Chapter 9

Medicare and Medicaid - the truth

The conservative media messaging machine and the conservative politicians screech Medicare and Medicaid are the reason we have such huge deficits. Another ridiculous lie. Oh please, we the 99% just have to keep telling the truth. The conservative politicians put two wars on the public credit card (no war bonds) or taxes, just borrowed money. Ten years later the wars are still on the public credit card. The conservative congress is still using borrowed money to give welfare to the top 1%. How irresponsible it that? It is bad enough they keep doing it, but to lie to the 99% of us and say that isn't why we have huge deficits is criminal. They also cut revenue more by giving all their rich friends welfare, and then they gave huge subsidies to drug companies (called it a benefit for the elderly)

The conservatives are borrowing money everyday to keep up two wars, welfare for the 1% and drug subsidies and they are blaming it on everything but the real culprits. Just because the conservatives keep screaming one thing, does not make it the truth. The huge deficits are caused by unfunded wars and drug company giveaways.

The simple truth.

Health care costs in America are the most expensive in the world. For all the money we spend we are not the healthiest in the world. All health insurance costs are going up, with so many having to pay higher co-pays. Health insurance companies are charging more and paying less out in claims. If we do not fundamentally change how we are paying for our health care we will continue to pay more money and get less service. We will not be any healthier.

Everyone who profits from the way healthcare is paid for now would like the current system to continue. As long as most insured people have no idea what any health care service or procedure costs. Nobody has idea how much drugs really cost, it will be extremely hard to drive down prices. As an example everything in a drug store has a price on it till you get to the prescription drug counter. The consumer does not know the cost of any drug other than what portion they pay. It is very hard to compare prices when you do not know the cost. The same thing happens when you go to a doctor's office. There is no chart with the prices. No price chart in a hospital admitting office. They have all kinds of information on how to pay, but not what anything costs while you are in the hospital.

Medicare and Medicaid have the lowest administrative costs of any insurance fund. The lobbyist who are paid by drug companies work hard for the drug companies to make sure that Medicare and Medicaid cannot use bargaining power to get much lower drug prices. Not being able to use the bargaining power of the volume of drugs they buy, significantly increases their costs That alone is driving up their costs, but nowhere near the costs of two wars on credit. The VA was not included in the drug subsidy business and they have much lower drug costs. So we know it can be done but the rich and powerful drug companies who are benefitting from the system they created, don't want you to know that.

The conservatives would like to do away with Medicare and Medicaid because it helps people and somebody is not making a profit. So they are launching a full out media assault telling everyone how expensive and awful they are. The 1% do not believe that the government should help anybody but the rich get richer. Remember winners and losers and they really dislike anybody who is in the middle. The insurance companies are in the business to make a great deal of money with the least output so they see Medicare and Medicaid as competition from them making them more money. The 1%, their conservative media messaging machine and conservative politicians do not care if people actually benefit from these services. Somewhere in another dimension the conservatives want us to believe someone who is 66years olds could somehow afford private health insurance. There is no private company that would even offer a plan that was affordable, but the conservative media messaging machine keeps screaming people need to responsible for themselves. The 1% and their conservative messaging machine does not want the government to help anybody but them. And the poor, well they don't really care about them after all it is their own fault that they are poor.

They don't have of these programs in Third World countries because they have the "survival of the richest" economy. Keep telling the truth. Don't stop.

~ ~ ~

Chapter 10

Taxing the rich will hurt the economy! Another famous lie

Let's just look at this, taxing the rich will hurt the economy. It is pure fantasy. The 1% can dress it up, scream, squeal, buy more politicians and media outlets to blast it from. The cold hard facts are easy to see. When the top 1% pays more taxes the rest of us do better. It has been that way all through out history. Let's say it again. When the top 1% pays more in taxes the rest of us do better! That did not hurt a bit to speak the truth. The economy grows more when the top 1% pays more taxes. So why aren't they paying more in taxes? Greedy behavior pure and simple. The top 1% only care about themselves and they have gamed the whole system in their favor. They do not need the rest of us and they do not want the system to change. Too bad the 99% of us have finally figured that out.

They can scream, yell, kick, do all the other things that selfish people do when they are caught being extremely selfish. The more they scream that they are job creators and the economy will crash if you tax them, the sillier they look. Like a spoiled child who sits in his room hoarding all their toys from everyone, so no one else can have any. They do look silly and childish.

With so many people here in America and around the world, it is really easy to see how this 1% is living so extremely well while the 99% are struggling. The difference between the 1% and the other 99% has never been wider. The 1% keeps telling us that this is the way it should be, they are entitled to what they have. The gap is so big that the top 1% of incomes have rose in the last 30 years by 277%, and everyone else has lost ground. The policy of "survival of the richest" has made this income gap so wide. So they keep shouting from all their paid politicians, all their media outlets and themselves that this is the way it is supposed to be, they have earned it.

No one earned this money without using our public infrastructure and public services. From the protected banks that keep their money, to roads, airports, sea ports, rail lines, skilled labor, or cheap labor, protected stock markets and a host of other infrastructure all around the world. They could not have made their fortunes without these public services.

Why does the economy do better when the top 1% is taxed at a much higher rate? It is really simple economics because when you tax the 1% at a much higher rate they will spend their money differently to lessen their tax burden. They will hire more workers and pay them better. The 1% and the corporations they own will offer their workers better benefits. The 1% and the corporations they own will invest in research and development all sorts of things to get that money back in the economy. Because it will be to their advantage. However when the 1% are given so much money tax free it does not go back into the economy. It does not trickle down! Let's say that again, it does NOT trickle down. That is why we all do better why the 1% are taxed at a higher rate. It is a great incentive to hire more workers (unemployment goes down), they increase wages and benefits (people have more money to spend) they expand factories (that really helps the economy). That money keeps flowing thru the economy at all different levels. Instead of just pouring into the top 1% is what we have now. History has shown us again and again that we have to give strong incentives for people to do the right thing. They do not do it on their own. That is why Third World Countries stay third world countries because they are divided by the 1% who have 99% of the wealth and the 99% who have so little.

If the conservative economic fantasy really worked like they say it will all Third World Countries would do better.

Nowhere in history does the overall economy do better when you keep pouring money into the top 1% and their corporations. We need to stop pouring money into the top 1%. The top 1% need to pay more in taxes and then all of us will all of us to do better. We cannot continue to give welfare to the top 1%." Survival of the richest", and the maddening tax policies fueling it needs to become so 20th century thinking. We need tax policies that will help all of us win the 21st Century. It is that simple.

~~~

Chapter 11

The real Spending Problem in Washington,DC

The conservatives keep blabbering that Washington,DC is spending too much money, over and over they blab that the spending problem is the Federal government. That is the lie. There is a spending problem in Washington. For many many years the conservatives politicians from Reagan to the current crop have spent like drunken sailors on shore leave when they had total control under Bush, and their wars are still on the public credit card, and the drug company give a ways. The conservative republicans still believe that spending apparently is okay, so is the welfare(tax breaks) for the rich. The spending the 1% and their conservative politicians don't like is anything that helps you and I the 99%! They keep shouting from all the usual places that the spending has to stop. Not the spending the 1% and their conservative media messaging machine like mind you, just the spending that helps the rest of us. They don't want to stop the borrowing and spending they do, just the spending that helps the 99% of us.

Let's really look at the spending that is doing the most damage to our democracy. It is not the spending that makes all of our lives better, safer, smarter, easier and comfortable. It is the anonymous money flowing into campaign coffers. Money that anybody, business, corporations, foreign government, you name it, they can give an unlimited amount of money to campaigns. This out of control, runaway spending will be the demise of our democracy. When the Supreme Court of the United States decided that they would rewrite all of the campaign finance rules with one decision, Citizens United. That has opened the flood gates so now the 1% can legally buy any politician. The 99% know which politicians they will buy, the ones who will keep them owning the goldmine while the rest of us get the shaft. (Boehner, Ryan ,McConnel)

This spending problem needs to be fixed. The way political campaigns are financed directly influences how politicians behave and vote. Just because the Supreme Court says you can do this, it does not mean we should allow our democracy to be corrupted.. The conservative messaging machine so influenced this decision and worked hard to have made this kind of corruption legal!!!! History will not be kind to this decision.

Each of us in the 99% needs to demand a much more ethical level of behavior and campaigns in our political system. If we the 99% really want these politicians to work for us, (instead of working for the people who fund their campaigns) we will have to change how these campaigns are funded. If we want our politicians to truly work for us, then we need to publicly fund their campaigns. The conservative messaging machine and their money is funding the new crop of "tea party" politicians(the most notorious, Gov Scott Walker, rep Paul Ryan, Sen Marco Rubio, Gov Ric Scott) They have made sure their money influenced and funded the campaigns of these extreme right wing politicians who clearly work for the 1% and their wants . The 99% of us have to put our money where our mouth is, simple economics. The politicians will then work for us.

This will be the cheapest money we ever spend.

The 99% need to change a few other election laws, but Citizens United needs to be stopped. The money that politicians have to raise to run for office is criminal. There is no way that the money they are given to fund their campaigns does not influence them. We are being naïve to think otherwise.

~ ~ ~

Chapter 12

The Magic of Polling

Polling is one of those things that all these "Think Tanks" have perfected. (Heritage Foundation, Hoover research group, and dozens more(They have figured out that if you want to influence the way people behave you need to really target those issues that bring an emotional response. Public opinion polls seem so innocent. They look like they are just trying to figure out what people are thinking.

We see polls every day. They poll about everything. So you wonder what is wrong with all this polling.

The questions-

Do you think the country is on the right track or wrong track?

Do you approve of congress?

Do you approve of the president's handling of the economy?

Do you believe that climate change is real?

All of these polls make you think about something that you did not think about until you saw the results. You would not on your own think, Is the country on the right track? But since the poll is out there, now you think about. So if the people polling wanted you to believe that this important they frame the question this way. Asking if you approve of congress gives you permission to disapprove of them. Asking if you approve of the president's handling of the economy is the same tactic, Now you can disapprove of the president. Asking if you believe that climate is real, plants the seeds of doubt that it is not real.

There is a lot of money spent on polling, and a great deal of time. Politicians make decisions based on these polls. This has become a new way to govern, ask people what they like, what they don't like, what they believe, what they don't believe, who do voters trust, who don't voters trust. Politicians can look like they know what they are doing to please their constituents.

Polling has replaced governance. The conservative messaging machine has perfected how to manipulated voters by convincing them that what the 1% has is okay with the 99% of us. How else would they have been able to do "Free Market","free trade", "trickle down", and all the other policies that are keeping the 1% with the biggest income disparity ever in our United States history

This has become a new way to govern, ask people what they want or don't want and give it to them. If you don't like what the other political party is doing, poll and get the public to support your position. This kind of polling is done so much it has actually hurts politicians ability to govern. We only have to look at the gridlock in congress and the US Senate

What the public needs is leaders who lead us where we need to go, whether we want to go there or not.(FDR, Winston Churchill) History is full of true leaders who put the common good ahead of personal ideology. We do not need leaders who follow behind us and say they are only doing what we want. They do this endless polling because they think this will help them to get re-elected again and again and stay in power as long as they want. They have been successful in staying in power, but very unsuccessful in leading us into the future. That would be real leadership, and instead they just keep giving people what they want, certainly the 1% who owns them. A true leader would of asked us to pay for the wars with war bonds, a true leader would of asked us to break our addiction to foreign oil to keep us from being held hostage by middle east terrorists.

What if instead we had leaders like the late Steve Jobs, who never believed in market research. He felt people did not know what they wanted until he gave it to them. What an orginal concept. Leaders who lead. What a radical idea.

Actually that is how leaders use to lead. They would take the citizens where they needed to go. Citizens don't always know where they need to go, and sometimes they don't want to go where they need to go.FDR with the New Deal, Social Security, Wilson the United Nations, many true leaders who have made our lives better in spite of the public opposition at that time.

This polling has become such a mainstay in American politics. If we are going to change they way we do politics in America we need to learn to recognized the purpose of polls. Always ask who is doing the polling and what do they hope to accomplish. Ask why they are polling? What will the results of the poll do? Don't ever just accept a poll. Question again and again why someone is asking these questions.

True leadership should not have to ask our opinions on what is the right thing to do. They should have an internal moral compass that points them in the direction of public good, not personal political ideology.

~ ~ ~

Chapter 13

The real crisis in the housing market the truth and lies

The truth, unsuspecting home buyers were misled into obtaining mortgages with very very low teaser interest rates. Unsuspecting homebuyers were also told that the eventual interest rate was not going to be very high. They were told not to worry the value of the house would increase and their incomes probably would increase. Life was good, the economy was buzzing right along. It would be a win win for everybody.

The mortgage brokers were making a killing selling these mortgages to homebuyers. Then stock brokers and bankers saw an incredible opportunity to take those mortgages bundle them together and sell them to Hedge Funds guaranteeing that the return would be 15% to 19%. No one could resist that kind of return, all the banks and funds wanted in on it.(the derivates market was booming ,credit default swaps, risky financial instruments)

Builders were building houses everywhere, even though we did not have a population explosion. There were seminars all over the country on how to make money flipping houses. Buy and sell real estate was the new money maker, next big thing

Realtors and lobbyists pressured congress and then president Bush to help make it easier for more people to buy houses. By the summer of 2008 the crisis reach a critical point.

While this housing bubble was inflating, the economy was losing steam fast. Oil prices started to destabilize, and gas was selling for $4 a gallon.

This was the beginning and the end will be a long time coming. The economy started collapsing. As gas prices rose, people realized they were having to make terrible choices. What do they pay and what bills did they not pay? Our economy was consumer driven, shopping was the number one economic activity that would keep the economy moving. When consumers were spending all their extra dollars on gas, rising food prices, they did not have money for frivolous shopping. This has had an incredible snow ball effect all across our economy. As demand for all sorts of goods stopped, the lay offs started and still continue today. Business's closed, plants closed, empty houses that have never been lived in were still for sale with no buyers. A perfect storm, homeowners could not pay their mortgages, especially the ones that went to a much higher interest rates. Many builders and investors who bought real estate with the intention of selling at an incredible profit were left instead with homes they could not sell. Thousands of building contractors went into bankruptcy.

The investors who held those mortgage securities with the promise of high returns were now losing value as more and more homeowners defaulted. The insurance companies who insured those securities were losing an incredible amount of money.

Meanwhile as more homes were foreclosed the values of homes have continued to drop. This had a severe impact on the housing market. People who could afford to pay their mortgages are now paying much more than the value of their house.

As more people go through all their resources to stay in their homes and the job market lags longer, more homes are going into foreclosure. There are many minority homeowners that still have unfair interests rates and they struggle.

During all of this the average American wages were stagnant and the money they were using to shop was borrowed on equity and credit cards. So many can only pay down on their debt instead of helping the economy. It will be very hard to ease the housing crisis with so many more homes than there are people to live in them, and if the values do not reflect what the local residents can really afford to pay for homes.

What makes this crisis so hard to solve is the millions of homeowners who still worry about their jobs. They know they are one medical emergency away from total ruin and there is no relief on the horizon for the 99% of us worried about the future.

~ ~ ~

Chapter 14

The last biggest lie - The tax burden is keeping business's from hiring

Oh please, just because the conservative messaging machine sounds like a broken record stuck on this phrase , doesn't make it so. They want the 99% of us to believe that if you tax business' they can't afford to hire more workers. If this was true that the tax burden was the reason for no one hiring, then those states that have given incredible incentives to businesses would be booming with low unemployment, but they are still not hiring. This is the wrong end of the problem. The conservatives want you to believe this so they can get more welfare for the top 1%. Businesses are not hiring because not enough people have any extra money to buy their products. It does not have anything to do with the tax burden. It is just another smoke screen to get out of paying taxes. They would like to get more free money and then they would think of another excuse when companies still don't hire.

Keep telling the conservative messaging machine and the politicians who work for them you will not fall for this lie. Because we have proof from all over the world in places that have no tax burden and they are still not hiring more workers.

The conservative messaging machine is still stuck on that broken record saying that we need to get back to the way things were. We need to get rid of the tax burden and companies will hire again and life will be good again.

The reason the economy is stuck is simple. When you send so many of our jobs overseas, to use that cheap labor and raw materials, and you get around all the pesky safety, environmental and labor laws. The people who can help spend our way out of this recession do not have any money to spend.

When the sole focus of the majority of companies is to just make the most money as possible at the expense of workers, and when enough companies do this. The end result is millions and millions of unemployed workers who do not have enough money for essentials, never mind what many consider to be frivolous shopping. They cannot spend any money, certainly money they no longer have.

There is no pent up demand to make companies want to make more products, and therefore need to hire more workers. This is simple economics of supply and demand.

Don't fall for this lie. The proof is everywhere around us. So many closed plants across the country. States all across the country have cut taxes because of this lie, and companies are still not hiring. You have to wonder have any of them taken economics 101. If people have money in their pockets they will spend it. When you take away their ability to make money, you take away their spending money. That is why the economy is in a recession, 70% of our economy is consumer driven. When those companies who were only concerned with how to make more money at the lowest overhead costs they shot themselves in their bank accounts. There are fewer and fewer consumers to spend money to get us out of this recession.

~ ~ ~

Chapter 15

Politics 101- we need to play and win

I hear all the time that people don't like politics. Personally I understand that politics is a blood sport and most people don't have a stomach for it. It doesn't matter if you want to or not. Politics is a part of all of our lives. Somebody made the political decision to put that highway thru your town, what kind of businesses could be on that highway, where the schools are in your community. Every decision that affects your lives was made by a group, a committee, a zoning board, state house, courthouse, congress. Somebody decided how clean our water had to be, how safe our cars have to be, how much your job was worth, what kind of benefits they had to give you, what kind of interest to pay on your money. Politics and political decisions are everywhere in our lives, so I remind people that some of us like to be making those decisions. If you really want to change the outcome of what is going on, it has to be done politically. That means some of you can work hard to run for public office and make those decisions and the rest need to make sure we are heard and make the politicians represent us again.

Everyone like games, sports, board, computer all kinds of games. Those of us in the 99% need to learn how to play this game that the 1% has mastered. It is the "war of words". We need to learn to use the same words, not their words, but our words. We need to learn how to take a stand, defend it and advance what we believe.

We the 99% need to learn to defend what is right and just. It is not fair that we all have to pay our fair share in taxes and be vilified when we need the services of our government. Articulate why it is right and just. Learn not to back down. The reason the conservatives with their messaging machine get their ideas out there and heard is because they all say the same thing over and over very loudly. They never get off message. That is one of the reasons all of their lies get traction. Remember they have invested thirty years, a great deal of money, time and effort in learning how to manipulate you the voter so they can advance these lies. They have done a brilliant job of stacking the economy in their favor to achieve "survival of the richest". Acknowledge that they have done this brilliantly. Look how much better they are doing than the rest of us. But, their gig is up, their time is almost done. "Survival of the richest" is so 20th century, it is time to go to the next level in economics.

Our strategy needs to be simple, clear and consistent.

* We the 99% need to tell them that they have played their hand brilliantly. It takes away some of the mystery and power they have over us.

* The 1% and their conservative messaging machine control a great deal of the mainstream media, we need to control the other media, social, and the internet media. The 99% have to use those numbers to get our message out there.

* The 1% got the gold mine and we got the shaft. Say it again and again. Loud and often.

* Tell our political leaders what we want and need. Shared prosperity. The ladder of success needs to be put back into reach.

* Greed (at all costs) is so 20th century, greed died with the collapsing economy

* Welfare(and unearned tax breaks) for the top 1% is the most expensive welfare in the world creating unearned profits

* Third World Countries have no taxes, regulations and limited government ,and yet they are still Third World Country. They have trickle down ,free market and free trade with no improvement in their economies just 1% and the 99%.

* The price to live and do business in our country is simple. Pay your fair share in taxes. The 99% of us cannot afford to carry the 1% any longer.

* If "trickle down" worked, there would be no 99%!!!!!

* If "free market" worked, there would be no 99%!!!!!

* If "free trade" worked, there would be no 99%!!!!!

So how do we go forward and win the 21st century?

The words we need to keep saying collectively to change this conversation.

Fair Trade (not free trade), Fair Markets, (not free markets), "survival of the richest" (not trickle down), welfare (tax breaks for the rich is welfare) fair taxes. Learn to be that broken record and not get off message.

There are some really easy solutions. Just think that if the "Horse and Buggy" industry had the lobbyists that business's do today. We would all be looking at the back end of horses! The businesses who are benefitting the most from the way things are do not want things to change. It is the simple survival tactics of those who currently hold the power today. They want us addicted to oil and oil products that we all use. If you never look at the world any other way than the way it is now of course the future looks bleak. Oil prices are getting higher and higher. Oil is such a dirty fuel to get out of the ground, refine, transport and when we burn it. It is a dirty fossil fuel. No doubt about it, but so many only look at the world being stuck on using this fuel source. Imagine a post oil world. It is easy to imagine we have all seen enough sci-fi movies to see that in the future we will have a different kind of energy. We need to head there and quickly. To continue on the energy path we are on short sighted and selfish.

We deserve the opportunity to leave a better world than we found to our children and grandchildren. How do we head down a different path? Of course there are a few obstacles, the media machine that has given us "survival of the richest" also would like us to stay addicted to oil. First they discredit all this climate change and global warming stuff going on around the world. They don't want any of us to stop using oil. Let's just imagine for a minute that we could past all that messaging and media screaming about how wonderful oil is. After all we just need to drill here there and everywhere for now.

Imagine instead that we put all those rocket scientists that don't have a shuttle program to work on anymore were given some new tasks. Imagine if we put them to work finding a way to double or triple the mileage on our personal vehicles. Imagine a way to redesign our engines in a practical way. Surely these highly trained and qualified engineers and scientists could do this. While some of them are working on this, what if we ask others to find alternative ways and energy to propel our vehicles. Power our homes and businesses. Surely there will be failures along the way, but imagine they can. We all have to believe in better. Whenever I would watch that little Mars Rover drive around Mars, I noticed there were no gas stations to keep it moving and none on the way to Mars. We can all imagine the future .We can do better. NASA, and the research and development they have created, was one of America's greatest moments of the 20th century. That pool of talented researchers needs to be a part of winning the 21st century and leading us away from our addiction of fossil fuels.

Imagine if our leaders asked us all to help with breaking this oil addiction. They could ask not to drive anywhere one day a week. Imagine if we were asked to stop using so many plastic products (they are all made of oil). There are so many little things that we could do, not using your clothes dryer as much, less driving. Stop using so much disposable stuff, especially plastic. Imagine if we all started believing in better. The hero we need is in the mirror. We all need to start calling on our better angels. We have to believe in better, not the same old same old. We have to get to work now. It is irresponsible for us not to act. We cannot leave this mess to the next generation. We all spend too much of our money on keeping these oil companies in business. Imagine if we all cut our gasoline bill in half or more. How much money would that leave in our pockets?

Imagine if we all could convince a few corporations to bring their jobs back to America. What if we could convince Wal-Mart to start purchasing" Made In America products". Just 10% for starters. That was Sam Walton's original goal when he started Wal-Mart. What a difference that would make.

Imagine if the new CEO of Apple came up with the revolutionary idea to bring the manufacturing of all the Apple products back to America. How great would that be for our economy. We all deserve better, we can demand better. The hero we are waiting for is in the mirror.

We need to win the 21st century, we cannot go back to the 19th century. We need new ideas, new energy, people who will question the status quo. We need people who have the courage to stand up to stupid thinking and tired ideas.

We have to get "it". We are not in this race alone. The two dark horses in this race are China and India. They know they cannot grow their economies by being addicted to oil. It is too expensive and they know it is not sustainable. Their incentive is greater than ours. They do not have an oil lobby trying to keep them in the 20th century. If one of those countries find a better source and type of energy, they will lead the world in exporting this technology. We will be left behind. We deserve better,

We need to win the 21st century on education. Our young people need to compete in the global world. We are 23rd in the world in education. The conservatives have gamed the system for "survival of richest" are the same ones who say we have to cut education, while giving more to the rich. Their kids go to private school, so they don't care about "public education". They want us to believe that teachers are overpaid villains and education dollars are wasted. Meanwhile China and India are making incredible investments in education. They know that investing in education pays off. Highly trained and educated workers are an asset to winning the 21st century. We have states here in America still arguing about evolution, instead of improving math and science scores. Our students deserve better so they can compete in the 21st century. Going back to the 19th century only benefits those who want more "survival of the richest".

We deserve better than the current mindset of "race to the bottom". The conservatives would like us all to believe that if we race to the bottom in wages, regulations, taxes, education, research and development that we will magically win the 21st century. We all need to remind the conservatives again and again that this thinking has given us "survival of the richest". We need to say this every chance you get, do not back down. Hold your ground. We all need to keep saying this till people start listening. It may take weeks, months. It has taken the conservatives 30 years to get us here, so we have a little time to change the mindset, but not much.

Chapter 16

Conclusion

We the 99% need to be the hero we are waiting for

All of us needs to "pay it forward." None of us got where we are on our own. Somebody before us built these roads, schools, hospitals, factories, airports, sea ports, knowing that the benefits and costs would be going to the next generations.

Why are we letting the 1% throw our children and up and coming generations under the bus. No other species will sacrifice the next generation deliberately like we do. All species know that for the species to survive you must protect and nurture the next generation. So why are we deliberately doing what nature tells us not to do. Why are we being so focused on today instead of tomorrow, next year, or next decade? Why aren't we looking ahead? Who is telling us we don't have to pay it forward? The conservatives want us all to focus on the short term, because they have found it keeps them in power.

The way we are living is not sustainable for very much longer. We are being extremely selfish to use up the planets resources for the now and today without a thought to what we are leaving generations and other species on the planet. Earth is home for many, many species besides humans, we seem to forget that. We have been duped in believing that buying more stuff, bigger houses and tons of disposable stuff our lives would be better. (many of us have learned to live without the stuff during this tough recession) There is a long term cost that we are ignoring and that future generations and other species will have to contend with. It is long past time to start having the conservation of how our species can achieve sustainability without destroying the planet. That will be one of the challenges of this century. That will be part of winning the 21st century. The country that starts working towards that goal will lead the way for the rest of the world. This will be "paying it forward".

The conservatives have spent the last 30 years undoing population sustainability. During the Carter administration in the 70's there was a global effort to assist families in family planning. When families control the size of their families it keeps them out of extreme poverty. The leading cause of poverty is having more children than you can afford to feed. When Reagan took office he signed the "gag order" which stopped funding for family planning around the world. The conservatives knew that when you had more poor people around the world there would be lots of cheap labor. So with a swipe of the pen the conservatives have caused more living, breathing children (millions and millions) to die by starvation and disease. Their policies and greed have led to a population explosion that will be very hard to sustain and feed in this century. They did get lots of cheap exploitable labor around the world. We will have to get serious about population size and sustainability. Our survival and the survival of every other species on this planet depends on it. If our generation cannot face this reality, then future generations will by default be responsible for tackling this issue.

The seeds that the conservatives have planted to keep the republicans in power and authority have born a very bitter fruit. We now have generations of people who have no respect for anybody that disagrees with them. Not only do these generations of young people who disrespect any one they don't like or agree with, they don't respect the conservatives either.

We have to realize we all have a common goal, and we all need to learn to compromise and help each other to win the 21st century. This planet is home to all us, not just some of us. What we do affects everyone.

Appendix

References

This has taken years to compile:

Books

"Politics Lost" by Joel Kleine

"Moral Politics" by George Lakoff

"Re-Inventing Government" by David Osborn & Ted Gaebler

"Words that Work" by Dr Frank Lutz

"The Political Brain" by Drew Weston

"Hot, Flat and Crowded" by Thomas Friedman

"Aftershock" by Robert Reich

Articles that were posted in major newspapers and online newsgroups

"The Secret Big-Money Takeover of America" by Robert Reich in Huffingtonpost 10/7/2010

"The Economy and D.C.: Republicans' Tax-cutting Fantasia" by NY Times 6/12/2011

"The Social Security/Medicare "Crisis" Is Really a Choice-Between..." by Richard Eskow 5/18/11

"When Wall St Rules-We get Wall Street Rules" by Dean Baker 8/21/2010

"The Seven Biggest Economic Lies" by Robert Reich 10/11/11 Huffingtonpost

"The Battle is Over Money, Not Philosophy" by Dean Baker 4/25/2011

"Wall Street Protests" by Sen Bernie Sanders 10/17/2011

"Don't Let Go of the Anger" by William Cohan 5/12/2011

"Why Grover Norquist is the Most Powerful Republican in America" by Eric Parker 3/9/11

"Debt Political Theatre Diverts Attention While America's Wealth is Stolen"by Dennis Kucinich

"Titanic Economics" by David Abromowitz 7/9/11

"Budgetary Deceit and Americas Decline" by Jeffery Sachs 7/23/11

"The Height of Congressional Irresponsibility and Once Again on the Backs of the Middle Class" by Leo Hendry Jr 7/5/2011

"States that Cut the Most Funding Lost the Most Jobs" analysis on 6/27/11 Huffingtonpost

"The Three Wings of the Republican Party " by Drew Weston 6/19/11

"The GOP's Latest Tax Gimmickry: Soak the Poor" by EJ Dionne Jr 10/26/11

"Bruce Bartlett, Ex-Reagan Economist: Idea That Deregulation Leads to Jobs "Just Made Up"

By Charles Babington 10/30/11

"Gingrich: Calamity Newt Asks the Right Questions" by Robert Borosage 5/17/11

"The Unwisdom Of Elites" by Paul Krugman 5/9/2011

"The Social Contract" by Paul Krugman 9/24/2011

"The 11 Words for 2011" by Frank Lutz 3/1/2011

"How Grover Norquist Hypnotized the GOP" by Governor Patrick Deval 6/30/2011

"The use of 9/11 to Consolidate Conservative Power" by George Lakoff 9/11/2011

"What Caused the Financial Crisis? The Big Lie goes Viral…" by Barry Ritholtz 11/20/2011

"The Billionaires Bankrolling the Tea Party" by Frank Rich 8/29/2010

"30 Billion in Millionaires Aide is Sheer Stupidity" by Sen Tom Colburn 11/15/2011

"How Did Our Oil Get Under Their Sand" by Dylan Ratigan 10/24/2011

"The Truth About Cats and Dogs" by Sharon Burrow 11/1/2011

"America's Mega-Mansions and Micro-cribs Grow Further Apart", by Fred Bernstein 11/1/2011

"Can We Avoid Locking Ourselves into Runaway Climate Change" by Kelly Rigg 11/15/2011

"Citizens United Fight: Constitutional Amendment Against Corporate Cash Introduced by House Democrats" by Haley Miller 11/15/2011

"Impartial Supreme Court Justices Raise Money for Opponents of Health Care Law" by Bod Edgar 11/13/2011

"Super Collusion: Will Obama and Capitol Dems Betray the Middle Class, Seniors and the Poor?"by Richard Eskow 11/12/2011

"Fed's Secrecy During Crisis Limits Effort to Stop Another" by Editors of Bloomberg News 11/29/11

"Understanding Where the Occupy Folks are Coming From" by Jared Bernstein 11/30/2011

"Occupy Elections, With a Simple Message" by George Lakoff 21/1/2011

"Wall Street is Already Occupied" by Jessie Eisinger 12/3/2011

"Nearly All Who Lost Jobs in Recession Are Worse Off Now: Poll" by Alexander Eicher 12/2/11

"Many have Little to no savings as retirement looms" by Matt Krantz 12/6/2011

The Heritage Foundation, website has their history and mission. You can sign up for "Morning Bell" e-mail and that is always the talking points for all conservatives and their media outlets. That is the number one driver of the conservative media machine.

Many economist, journalists, politicians have been saying and documenting was has been going on for over 30 years, I have just connected the dots and put it into language you can easily understand. Knowledge is power. Everyone needs to pay attention to what politicians are doing, elections do have consequences.